The Wisdom of The Cloud of Unknowing

The Wisdom of The Cloud of Unknowing

Compiled and introduced by
Bradley Holt

This edition copyright © 1999 Lion Publishing

Published by
Lion Publishing plc
Sandy Lane West, Oxford, England
www.lion-publishing.co.uk
ISBN 0 7459 3978 3

First edition 1999
10 9 8 7 6 5 4 3 2 1 0

All rights reserved

A catalogue record for this book is available
from the British Library

Typeset in 12.5/13 Venetian 301
Printed and bound in Singapore

Artwork: Amanda Barlow
Designer: Philippa Jenkins

Text Acknowledgments

The Cloud of Unknowing, ed. James Walsh, SJ, New York: Paulist Press, 1981.

Picture Acknowledgments

cover: MS. Douce 293, fol. 87v; The Bodleian Library, University of Oxford
1: MS. Douce 366, fol. 23r; The Bodleian Library, University of Oxford
2: All Souls College MS. 7, fol. 38v; The Warden and Fellows of All Souls College, Oxford
9: MS. Douce 366, fol. 64v; The Bodleian Library, University of Oxford
13: All Souls College MS. 7, fol. 91r; The Warden and Fellows of All Souls College, Oxford
19: MS. Douce 366, fol. 31r; The Bodleian Library, University of Oxford
22: MS. Bodley 264, pt 1, fol. 88v; The Bodleian Library, University of Oxford
25: All Souls College MS. 7, fol. 103r; The Warden and Fellows of All Souls College, Oxford
27: MS. Bodley 264, pt 1, fol. 88v; The Bodleian Library, University of Oxford
33: All Souls College MS. 7, fol. 26r; The Warden and Fellows of All Souls College, Oxford
37: All Souls College MS. 7, fol. 89r; The Warden and Fellows of All Souls College, Oxford
41: MS. Douce 366, fol. 12r; The Bodleian Library, University of Oxford
43: MS. Douce 366, fol. 65v; The Bodleian Library, University of Oxford
48: All Souls College MS. 7, fol. 116r; The Warden and Fellows of All Souls College, Oxford

Contents

Introduction 6

The Exercise Above All Others 9

The Two Clouds 19

The Dart of Longing Love 27

The Use of the Exercise 33

INTRODUCTION

The Cloud of Unknowing is a protest against arrogant theologians and a handbook for all who seek to know God through love rather than through knowledge.

What if the basis of the spiritual life could be simplified into a single exercise? What if this exercise could be practised in a moment of time? What if it could be accomplished by anyone at any time? The exercise, to put it briefly, is to reach out to God in love. The author believes that if one does this constantly one's soul will be purified, virtues will develop, one will love others and have a foretaste of heaven.

But knowing God through love turns out to be more complex than it first appears. The author points out that reaching God is not within human ability, but is possible only by God's grace. Grace is a kind of 'super-love' whereby God reaches out to us, even when we do not want to reach God. It is a simple exercise that the author teaches; one does not need to be a monk or a nun to practise it. But the author insists that one must confess one's sins, practise the exercise continuously and avoid the errors which he has observed as a spiritual guide and counsellor. It would be a mistake to take this exercise out of the context of the scriptures, sacraments and good spiritual direction.

One of the best-loved writings in the English mystical tradition, *The Cloud of Unknowing* remains a puzzle. No one has yet discovered the name of its author. The book is a long letter from a seasoned spiritual counsellor to a beginner in the contemplative life, and it is thought that the author was a hermit, perhaps a Carthusian priest, writing in the late 1300s.

The author is well-read in theology, but, wearing his learning lightly, rarely refers to the names of the theologians whose thought lies just under the surface of his writing. He follows the tradition of apophatic spirituality, classically expressed by another anonymous writer, commonly known as Dionysius, from the fifth century. The apophatic tradition asserts that if we are to know God through our own experience we must leave behind all our concepts, doctrines and images of God. This is the meaning of the title, *The Cloud of Unknowing*. The true nature of God is hidden from us by the cloud, yet love can penetrate even this darkness. What this author calls a cloud, St John of the Cross later refers to as the 'dark night of the soul'. In our own day, the apophatic tradition is practised as 'centring prayer' and advocated by those who combine Christian and Zen meditation.

This is not a book to answer every question. It focuses carefully on contemplative prayer. Today many of us would insist that even a contemplative must involve herself or himself in the problems of the world, as did Thomas Merton. But the core of that contemplative life is described nowhere better than in this book. The author is practical, down-to-earth, compassionate and experienced.

The Prologue of the book urgently asks that it be read only by those who are serious about the contemplative life, and that it be read 'right through' to avoid the misunderstandings which may occur from short selections. In accordance with the author's request, and for your own benefit, I urge you to read the whole of *The Cloud* after sampling this modest selection.

BRADLEY HOLT

THE EXERCISE ABOVE ALL OTHERS

I

THE DESIRE FOR GOD

Press on, then, with speed, I pray you. Look ahead now and never mind what is behind; see what you still need, and not what you have; for this is how meekness is most quickly won and defended. Now you have to stand in desire, all your life long, if you are to make progress in the way of perfection. This desire must always be at work in your will, by the power of almighty God and by your own consent.

One point I must emphasize: he is a jealous lover and allows no other partnership, and he has no wish to work in your will unless he is there alone with you, by himself. He asks no help, but only you yourself. His will is that you should simply gaze at him, and leave him to act alone. Your part is to keep the windows and the door against the inroads of flies and enemies.

And if you are willing to do this, all that is required of you is to woo him humbly in prayer, and at once he will help you.

Chapter II

2
GOD ALONE

Lift up your heart to God with a humble impulse of love; and have himself as your aim, not any of his goods. Take care that you avoid thinking of anything but himself, that there is nothing for your reason or your will to work on except himself. Do all that in you lies to forget all the creatures that God ever made, and their works, so that neither your thought nor your desire be directed or extended to any of them, neither in general nor in particular. Let them alone and pay no attention to them. This is the work of the soul that pleases God most.

Chapter III

3

THE CLOUD

We cannot know how wonderfully all people dwelling on earth are helped by this exercise… Do not hang back, then, but labour in it until you experience the desire.

For when you first begin to undertake it, all that you find is a darkness, a sort of cloud of unknowing; you cannot tell what it is, except that you experience in your will a simple reaching out to God. This darkness and cloud is always between you and your God, no matter what you do, and it prevents you from seeing him clearly by the light of understanding in your reason, and from experiencing him in sweetness of love in your affection. So set yourself to rest in this darkness as long as you can, always crying out after him whom you love. For if you are to experience him or to see him at all, insofar as it is possible here, it must always be in this cloud and in this darkness.

Chapter III

4

GOD'S IMAGE AND LIKENESS

He fits himself exactly to our souls by adapting his Godhead to them; and our souls are fitted exactly to him by the worthiness of our creation after his image and his likeness. He, by himself alone, and no one but he, is fully sufficient, and much more so, to fulfil the will and the desire of our souls.

Chapter IV

5

THE LOVING POWER

Now all rational creatures, angels and men alike, have in them, each one individually, one chief working power, which is called a knowing power, and another chief working power called a loving power; and of these two powers, God, who is the maker of them, is always incomprehensible to the first, the knowing power. But to the second, which is the loving power, he is entirely comprehensible in each one individually; insomuch that one loving soul of itself, because of love, would be able to comprehend him who is entirely sufficient, and much more so, without limit, to fill all the souls of men and angels that could ever exist. This is the everlastingly wonderful miracle of love, which shall never have an end. For he shall ever work it and shall never cease to do so. Let him understand it who can do so by grace; for the experience of this is endless happiness, and its contrary is endless suffering.

Chapter IV

6

PRECIOUS TIME

So take good care of time, therefore, and how you spend it. Nothing is more precious than time. In one small particle of time, little as it is, heaven can be won and lost. This is a sign that time is precious: God, who is the giver of time, never gives two particles of time together, but one after the other. This is because he refuses to reverse the order and the regular chain of causes in his creation. Time is made for man, not man for time…

So love Jesus, and everything that he has is yours. By his Godhead he is the maker and giver of time. By his manhood he is truly the keeper of time. And by his Godhead and manhood together he is the truest judge and accountant of the spending of time. Knit yourself, then, to him by love and by faith.

Chapter IV

7

DIVINE SPARKS

Pay careful heed, then, to this exercise, and to the wonderful way in which it works within your soul. For when rightly understood, it is nothing else than a sudden impulse, one that comes without warning, speedily flying up to God as the spark flies up from the burning coal. Marvellous also are the number of such impulses that can take place in one hour in a soul that is properly disposed for the exercise. Yet in one stirring out of all these, a man can suddenly and perfectly have forgotten every created thing. And equally quickly, after each impulse, because of the corruption of the flesh, the soul falls down again to some thought or some deed done or undone. But what matter? For straightaway it rises again as suddenly as it did before.

Chapter IV

8

THE WORK OF DEVOTION

And so, you may ask, where precisely is the labour? The work consists in the treading down of the awareness of all the creatures that God ever made, and in keeping them under the cloud of forgetting, as we mentioned before. Here is all the labour; for this, with the help of grace, is man's work. And the other beyond this, the impulse of love, this is the work of God alone. So press on with your own work, and he, I promise you, will certainly not fail in his.

Press on, then, earnestly, and show your mettle. Do you not see how he is standing waiting for you? For shame! Labour earnestly for a little while, and you will soon find rest from the severity and the hardship of that work. For though it is hard and constraining in the beginning, when you have no devotion, nevertheless afterwards, when you have devotion, it shall become very restful and very easy for you, though it was so hard before. Then you shall have very little labour, or none at all. For then God will work sometimes all by himself; but not always nor even for a long time together, but when it pleases him and as it pleases him; then it will seem to you a joyful thing to leave him to get on with it.

Then perhaps it will be his will to send out a ray of spiritual light, piercing this cloud of unknowing between you and him, and he will show you some of his secrets, of which man may not or cannot speak. Then you shall feel your affection all aflame with the fire of his love, far more than I know how to tell you or may or wish to at this time. For I dare not take it upon me to speak with my blabbing, fleshly tongue of the work that belongs to God alone; and, to put it briefly, even though I dared so to speak I would not wish to. But I am very pleased to speak to you of the work that falls to man, when he feels himself moved and helped by grace; for it is less hazardous to speak of this than of the other.

Chapter XXVI

THE TWO CLOUDS

Spiritual Darkness

Now when I call this exercise a darkness or a cloud, do not think that it is a cloud formed out of the vapours which float in the air, or a darkness such as you have in your house at night, when your candle is out. For such a darkness or such a cloud you can certainly imagine by subtle fancies, as though it were before your eyes, even on the clearest day of summer; and likewise, on the darkest night of winter, you can imagine a clear shining light. But leave such falsehood alone. I mean nothing of that sort. When I say 'darkness', I mean a privation of knowing, just as whatever you do not know or have forgotten is dark to you, because you do not see it with your spiritual eyes. For this reason, that which is between you and your God is termed not a cloud of the air, but a cloud of unknowing.

Chapter IV

10

CLOUD OF UNKNOWING; CLOUD OF FORGETTING

But now you put me a question and say: 'How might I think of him in himself, and what is he?' And to this I can only answer thus: 'I have no idea.'

For with your question you have brought me into that same darkness, into that same cloud of unknowing where I would you were yourself. For a man may, by grace, have the fullness of knowledge of all other creatures and their works, yes, and of the works of God's own self, and he is well able to reflect on them. But no man can think of God himself. Therefore, it is my wish to leave everything that I can think of and choose for my love the thing that I cannot think. Because he can certainly be loved, but not thought. He can be taken and held by love, but not by thought.

Therefore, though it is good at times to think of the kindness and worthiness of God in particular, and though this is a light and a part of contemplation, nevertheless, in this exercise, it must be cast down and covered over with a cloud of forgetting. You are to step above it stalwartly but lovingly, and with a devout, pleasing, impulsive love strive to pierce that darkness above you. You are to smite upon that thick cloud of unknowing with a sharp dart of longing love. Do not leave that work for anything that may happen.

Chapter VI

11

REACHING OUT TO GOD

Therefore, when you set yourself to this exercise, and experience by grace that you are called by God to it, then lift up your heart to God by a humble impulse of love... For a simple reaching out directly towards God is sufficient, without any other cause except himself.

If you like, you can have this reaching out wrapped up and enfolded in a single word. So as to have a better grasp of it, take just a little word, of one syllable rather than of two; for the shorter it is the better it is in agreement with this exercise of the spirit. Such a one is the word 'God' or the word 'love'. Choose which one you prefer, or any other according to your liking – the word of one syllable that you like best. Fasten this word to your heart, so that whatever happens it will never go away. This word is to be your shield and your spear, whether you are riding in peace or in war. With this word you are to beat upon this cloud and this darkness above you.

Chapter VII

Action and Contemplation

Next, you ask me why you should put down such thoughts under the cloud of forgetting, since it is true that they are good of their kind, and when well used they do you so much good and greatly increase your devotion. My answer is that you must clearly understand that there are two kinds of lives in holy Church. One is the active life, and the other is the contemplative life. The active life is the lower and the contemplative life is the higher. The active life has two degrees, a higher and a lower; and the contemplative life also has two degrees, a lower and a higher. Further, these two lives are so joined together that though in part they are different, neither of them can be lived fully without having some part in the other. For the higher part of the active life is the same as the lower part of the contemplative life. Hence, a man cannot be fully active unless he is partly a contemplative, nor can he be fully contemplative here below unless he is in some way active. It is the nature of the active life both to be begun and ended in this life. Not so, however, of the contemplative life, which is begun in this life and shall last without end.

Chapter VIII

13

LOVE LIFTED UP

One thing I must tell you. This blind impulse of love towards God for himself alone, this secret love beating on this cloud of unknowing, is more profitable for the salvation of your soul, more worthy in itself, and more pleasing to God, and to all the saints and angels in heaven; yes, and of more use to all your friends both bodily and spiritually, whether they are alive or dead. And it is better for you to experience this spiritually in your affection than it is to have the eye of your soul opened in contemplation either in seeing all the angels and the saints in heaven, or in hearing all the mirth or the melody that is amongst those who are in bliss…

So lift up your love to that cloud; or rather, if I am to speak more truthfully, let God draw your love up to that cloud; and try, through the help of his grace, to forget every other thing.

Chapter IX

The Dart of Longing Love

14

THAT BLIND IMPULSE OF LOVE

If, then, you are determined to stand and not to fall, never cease from your endeavour, but constantly beat with a sharp dart of longing love upon this cloud of unknowing which is between you and your God. Avoid thinking of anything under God and do not leave this exercise no matter what happens. For it alone, of itself, destroys the root and the ground of sin. No matter how much you fast, or keep watch, no matter how early you rise, no matter how hard your bed... The impulse and tendency to sin would still be in you.

Yes, and more than this. No matter how much you were to weep and sorrow for your sins, or for the passion of Christ, or be ever so mindful of the joys of heaven, what would it profit you? Certainly it would be of great good, great help, great gain and great grace. But in comparison with that blind impulse of love, there is little it can or may do.

Chapter XII

Two Causes of Humility

In itself, humility is nothing else but a man's true understanding and awareness of himself as he really is. It is certain that if a man could truly see and be conscious of himself as he really is, he would indeed be truly humble. There are two causes of this meekness: one is the foulness, wretchedness and weakness into which a man has fallen by sin. As long as he lives in this life, no matter how holy he is, he must always experience this in some measure.

The other is the superabundant love and worthiness of God himself. At the sight of this, all nature trembles, all learned men are fools, and all the saints and angels are blinded; so much so that were it not for the wisdom of his Godhead, whereby due proportion is set between their contemplation and their natural and grace-given capacity, I would be at a loss to say what would happen to them.

This second cause of humility is perfect, because it will last for ever.

Chapter XIII

PERFECT HUMILITY

So you who set yourself to be a contemplative... choose rather to be humbled under the wonderful height and worthiness of God, which is perfect, than under your own wretchedness, which is imperfect. That is to say, take care that you make the worthiness of God the object of your special contemplation, rather than your own wretchedness. For they who are perfectly humble shall never lack anything, neither corporal nor spiritual. The reason is that they have God, in whom is all abundance; whoever has him, indeed, as this book says, needs nothing else in this life.

Chapter XXIII

17

THE MEANING OF CHARITY

We have said that humility is subtly and perfectly contained in this little blind impulse of love as it beats upon this dark cloud of unknowing, with all other things put down and forgotten. The same is to be understood of all the other virtues, and particularly of charity. We are to understand that charity means nothing else than the love of God for himself above all creatures, and the love of man equal to the love of yourself for God's sake... In this exercise the perfect apprentice does not ask to be released from pain or for his reward to be increased; in a word, he asks for nothing but God himself; so much so that he takes no account or regard of whether he is in pain or in joy, but only that the will of him whom he loves be fulfilled.

Chapter XXIV

No Special Regard

Experience shows that in this exercise the second, lower branch of charity, that for your fellow-Christian, is truly and perfectly fulfilled. For the perfect worker here has no special regard for any individual, whether he is kinsman or stranger, friend or foe. For he considers all men alike as his kinsmen, and no man a stranger to him. He considers all men his friends and none his foes. So much so that he considers all those that cause him pain and do him mischief in this life to be his very special friends, and he considers that he is being moved to wish them as much good as he would to the dearest friend he has.

Chapter XXIV

The Use of the Exercise

19

THE WORK OF GOD

If you ask me by what means you are to come to the practice of this exercise, I beseech almighty God out of his great grace and great courtesy to teach you himself. For it is right for me to let you know that I cannot tell you; and no wonder. Because this is the work of God alone, brought about in a special way in whatever soul that pleases him, without any merit on its part. For without this divine work neither saint nor angel can ever hope even to desire it. And I believe that our Lord will deign to effect this work in those that have been habitual sinners, particularly and as often, yes, and perhaps even more particularly and more often, in those who have been habitual sinners, than in others who, comparatively speaking, have never caused him great grief. It is his will to do this because he wishes to be seen as all-merciful and almighty; he wishes us to see that he works as it pleases him, where it pleases him and when it pleases him.

Chapter XXXIV

20

LET IT BE

To put it more clearly, let it do with you and lead you as it will. Let it be the one that works; you must simply consent to it. Simply look at it, and just let it be. Do not interfere with it, as though you wished to help it on, lest you spoil it all. Try to be the wood and let it be the carpenter; the house, and let it be the husbandman dwelling in the house. During this time be blind, and cut away all desire of knowing; for this will hinder you more than it will help you. It is enough for you that you feel moved in love by something, though you do not know what it is; so that in this affection you have no thought of anything in particular under God, and that your reaching out is simply directed to God.

If this is the way of it, then trust steadfastly that it is God alone who moves your will and your desire: he alone, entirely of himself, without any intermediary, either on his part or on yours.

Chapter XXXIV

READ, REFLECT, PRAY

Nevertheless, there are certain preparatory exercises which should occupy the attention of the contemplative apprentice: the lesson, the meditation and the petition. They may be called, for a better understanding, reading, reflecting and praying…

God's word, whether written or spoken, is like a mirror. The spiritual eye of your soul is your reason. Your spiritual face is your consciousness. And just as your bodily eyes cannot see where the dirty mark is on your bodily face without a mirror, or without someone else telling you where it is, so with your spiritual faculties. Without reading or listening to God's word, it is not possible for the understanding, when the soul is blinded by habitual sin, to see the dirty mark on his consciousness. It follows, then, that when a person sees in the bodily or the spiritual mirror, or knows by the information he gets from someone else, just where the dirty mark is on his bodily or spiritual face, he goes to the well to wash it off – and not before. Now if this mark is a particular sin, the well is holy Church and the water is confession, with all its elements. And if the mark is simply the blind root with the impulse to sin, then the well is the merciful God and the water is prayer, with all its elements.

And so you can see that beginners and proficients cannot come to proper reflection without previous reading or listening, or to prayer without previous reflection.

Chapter XXXV

22

PRAYERS THAT PIERCE HEAVEN

Just as this little word 'fire' suddenly beats upon and jars most effectively the ears of the bystanders, it is the same with the little word, whether spoken or thought or even obscurely conceived in the depth, or we may call it the height, of the spirit. (For in the spiritual realm, height and depth, length and breadth are all the same.) And thus it bursts upon the ears of almighty God much more than any long psalm mumbled away in an inarticulate fashion. And this is why it is written that a short prayer pierces heaven.

Chapter XXXVII

TWO WORDS

We must therefore pray in the height and the depth, the length and the breadth of our spirit; and not in many words but in a little word of one syllable. What shall this word be?...

Prayer in itself is nothing but a devout reaching out directly to God, in order to attain the good and to do away with evil. And since every evil is comprehended in sin, either as its effect or as sin itself, when we wish to pray with concentration for the removal of evil, we must neither say nor think, nor mean anything else, using no other words but this little word 'sin'. And if we desire with all our intent to pray for the attainment of any good, let us cry either verbally or in thought or desire, using nothing else, nor any other word, but this word 'God'. Because in God is contained all good, both as effect or as Being.

Chapter XXXIX

24

TAKE CARE OF YOURSELF

If you ask me the further question, how you are to apply discretion to this exercise, I answer and say, 'none at all!' In all your other activities you are to have discretion, in eating and drinking, in sleeping, and in protecting your body from the extremes of heat and cold, in the length of time you give to prayer or reading or to conversation with your fellow Christians. In all these things you are to observe moderation, avoiding excess and defect. But in this exercise there is no question of moderation; I would prefer that you should never leave off as long as you live.

I do not say that you should persevere in it with the same vigour; for that is not possible. Sometimes sickness or other disorders of body or of soul, and many other necessities of nature, will greatly hinder you, and often pull you down from the height of this exercise. But I do say that you should always be either doing it or preparing for it; that is to say either actually or in intention. So for the love of God, beware of sickness as much as it is possible for you. Insofar as you can, never be the cause of your physical weakness. For it is true what I say: this work demands a great tranquillity, and a clean bill of health as well in body as in soul. So for the love of God, govern yourself wisely in body and in soul, and keep in good health as much as possible.

Chapter XLI

25

SPIRITUAL SORROW

So you must destroy all knowing and feeling of every kind of creature, but most especially of yourself… What remains between you and your God is a simple knowing and feeling of your own being.

Next you will ask me how you can destroy this simple awareness and experience of your own being… My answer to you is this: without a very special grace which God gives out of his absolute bounty, and along with it a corresponding capacity on your part for receiving this grace, this simple awareness and experience of your being can in no way be destroyed.

This capacity is nothing else but a strong and profound spiritual sorrow… All men have reason for sorrow; but he who knows and feels that he exists has a very special experience of sorrow…

Every soul must possess and experience in itself this sorrow and this desire, either in this way or in another way as God will grant in the teaching of his spiritual disciples, according to his good pleasure and their corresponding capacity, in body and in soul, in degree and disposition, before they can be perfectly united to God in perfect charity, insofar as this union can be possessed in this life, if God will grant it.

Chapters XLIII, XLIV

26

A GAME

So for the love of God, take very great care in this exercise not to strain yourself immoderately or overtax the heart in your breast. The exercise calls for spiritual skill rather than brute strength. To work more skilfully means to work with humility and in the spirit; if you force it, the work is merely in the body and the senses…

And I advise you to play some sort of game, so that you can do all that is possible to contain these great and boisterous movements of your spirit: as though you did not wish him to know in any way how you desire to see him and have him or experience him. Perhaps you think this is somewhat foolishly and childishly spoken. But I am certain that whoever had the grace to do and feel as I say would find that this game was well worth playing with him, even as the father plays with the child, kissing and embracing it.

Chapter XLVI

SWEET EXPERIENCES

We must focus all our attention on this meek stirring of love in our will. And with regard to all other sweetnesses and consolations, sensible or spiritual, no matter how pleasing they are, no matter how holy, we should have a sort of heedlessness. If they come, welcome them; but do not depend too much on them because of your weakness; for to continue for long in those sweet experiences and tears is a great drain on your strength. It may be that you will be moved to love God simply for their sake. You will know that this is so if you grumble overmuch when they are withdrawn. If this is your experience, then your love is not yet either chaste or perfect. For when love is chaste and perfect, though it is content that the bodily senses be nourished and consoled through the presence of these experiences and tears, yet it does not grumble. It is well satisfied to do without them, if such be God's will.

Chapter L

28

PRESENT IN SPIRIT

My counsel is to take care that you are in no sense within yourself. To put it briefly, I would have you be neither outside yourself, above yourself, nor behind, nor on one side or the other.

'Where, then,' you will say, 'am I to be? According to your reckoning, nowhere!' Now indeed you speak well, for it is there that I would have you. Because nowhere bodily is everywhere spiritually. Take good care, then, that your spiritual exercise is nowhere bodily. Then, wherever the object is on which you set yourself to labour in the substance of your mind, truly you are there in spirit, as truly as your body is in the place where you dwell bodily.

Chapter LXVIII

Spiritual Counsel

But if you think that this way of working is not according to your bodily or spiritual disposition, you can leave it and take another safely and without reproach, as long as it is with good spiritual counsel. And in that case I beseech you that you will hold me excused. For truly my purpose in writing this book was to help you to make progress according to my own simple knowledge. That was my intention. So read it over two or three times; and the oftener the better, and the more you shall understand of it; so that, perhaps, if some sentence was very difficult for you to understand at the first or second reading, it will then seem to you easy enough.

Chapter LXXIV

30

A FINAL BLESSING

Farewell, spiritual friend, in God's blessing and mine. And I beseech almighty God that true peace, sane counsel and spiritual comfort in God, with abundance of grace, always be with you and with all those who on earth love God. Amen.

Chapter LXXV